THE LAW AND YOUR FAMILY

YOUR LEGAL RIGHTS

G. S. PRENTZAS

ROSEN
PUBLISHING

New York

Published in 2015 by The Rosen Publishing Group, Inc.
29 East Street, New York, NY 10010

Expert Reviewer: Lindsay A. Lewis, Esq.

Library of Congress Cataloging-in-Publication Data

Prentzas, G. S., author.
The law and your family: your legal rights/G.S. Prentzas.
    pages cm.—([Know your rights])
Includes bibliographical references and index.
ISBN 978-1-4777-8012-1 (library bound)—
ISBN 978-1-4777-8013-8 (pbk.)—
ISBN 978-1-4777-8014-5 (6-pack)
1. Domestic relations—United States—Juvenile literature.
2. Separation (Law—United States—Juvenile literature. 3. Custody of children—United States—Juvenile literature. I. Title.
KF505.P74 2015
346.7301'5—dc23
                                                              2014021406

Manufactured in the United States of America

CONTENTS

INTRODUCTION

I magine that you have recently separated from your husband or live-in boyfriend. Your relationship had been slowly falling apart for more than a year. After a really heated argument that ended with him slapping you hard in the face, you finally had enough. When he went to work the next day, you moved out of the apartment you shared, taking the young child you had together with you.

Your ex started sending you text messages, saying that he loves you and wants you and the child back. When you ignore his messages, he sends more texts, writing that you "will be sorry" that you left him and that you "don't deserve" to keep the child. The texts frighten you, and you want to make his threats stop. You need help for yourself and your child. What should you do?

People often face conflicts and legal problems involving their families. Family law covers issues ranging from marriage and divorce to the rights of minors and child abuse. Because strong personal relationships are usually involved, family conflicts can be stressful and difficult to resolve.

If you, or a friend, are facing a difficult issue related to family law, the legal system can provide a solution to the problem.

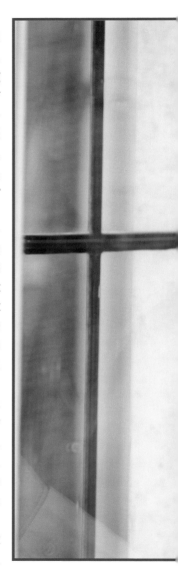

If you are receiving threatening texts from someone—including a relative, spouse, girlfriend, boyfriend, or ex—the legal system can help stop the harassment.

Because knowledge is power, you need to research the laws that apply to the situation. To resolve the problem, you or your friend must navigate the legal system and use it to get what you want.

Knowing the law and using the legal system will help you no matter what your family-law problem is. In the imaginary case above, you could go to your local county courthouse and fill out an application for a protective order. A judge would issue a temporary protective order that forbids your ex from having contact with you or your child. The court would schedule a hearing. At the hearing, the judge would weigh the evidence and perhaps issue a permanent protective order.

State laws also make domestic violence and threatening behavior crimes. You could file a complaint against your ex with the police. They would investigate your complaint and perhaps arrest your ex, charging him with assault or other crimes.

For people caught up in family-law problems, state agencies and community organizations offer many services, from child-abuse hotlines or temporary shelter for victims of domestic violence, to mental-health counseling or free legal advice on divorce, child support, and other issues. Taking advantage of these services is another smart way to handle a family-law problem. This book describes the basics of family law in the United States.

CHAPTER 1

GETTING HITCHED

Cristin Z. and her fiancé got a mortgage to buy a condo in San Francisco together and moved into the apartment. About a month before the wedding, the couple broke up. Because they would lose money if they sold the condo and paid off their mortgage, Cristin offered to let her ex have the apartment if she could keep the engagement ring. He did not want to keep making the mortgage payments on his own, so her ex rejected the offer. He also told her he was going to sue her to get the ring back. If you were in Cristin's shoes, would you know what to do?

MARRIAGE BASICS

Marriage has been a basic part of life since ancient times. Today, more than two million people in the United States get married each year. You might think of marriage as a romantic bond between two people, and in most cases, you would be right. By getting married, a couple promises to make a lifelong commitment to share their lives. However, marriage also has important legal effects. When you get married, you gain many legal rights and benefits, but take on certain responsibilities.

Marriage isn't just about love and commitment. Important legal rights and duties come with marriage. You must also meet your state's legal requirements for marriage in order to have a legal union.

Marriage is defined as the legal union of two people. To get married, you must meet certain legal requirements. These requirements vary from state to state, but there are some general rules. You must be old enough to enter into a legal contract under state law; the minimum age is usually eighteen years old. You cannot be too closely related to your intended spouse. That means you cannot marry your sibling or half-sibling; a parent, grandparent, or great-grandparent; your child, grandchild, or great-grandchild; or an aunt, uncle, niece, or nephew.

To get married, both partners must understand what they're doing and what the consequences of their marriage would be. For example, you must be sober at the time of the marriage ceremony. Neither you nor your partner can be so intoxicated that you do not knowingly enter the marriage contract; otherwise, the marriage would be voidable (that is, one party could dissolve the marriage). Neither partner can already be married to someone else; if you marry someone who is already married, your marriage would be void (legally nonexistent). Other factors can also make a marriage void or voidable.

Some states require both partners to have a blood test, which checks for venereal disease and measles. The blood tests may also reveal sickle-cell anemia or another genetic disease. You will not be tested for HIV, but in some states, the person who tests you will provide you with information about HIV and AIDS.

HOW TO GET MARRIED

For a marriage to be legal, you must obtain a marriage license. You can get a marriage license at a county clerk's office in the state where you want to be married. It usually requires a fee. To prevent hasty marriages, some states

TEEN MARRIAGE

In almost all states, a person must be eighteen years old to marry. Most states allow people younger than eighteen to marry if they have the consent of their parents. Parental consent usually requires either a written letter or a copy of a consent form signed by a parent or both parents. In some states, the parent or parents must either sign the consent form at the office of the county clerk issuing the marriage license or be present at the clerk's office when the marriage application is submitted. In most states, the minimum age for a marriage with parental consent is sixteen. Some states allow a person who is younger than sixteen to marry with parental consent and a judge's permission. This is extremely rare and usually happens only when the prospective bride is pregnant.

Many people get married in a religious ceremony, and other couples choose a civil ceremony. Both types of ceremonies result in legal marriages in almost all cases.

make you wait a few days before the license is issued. In some states, you might have to wait a few days after you receive the license before you can tie the knot.

Marriage requires a ceremony. A religious authority can conduct a religious ceremony. A judge or justice of the peace usually performs a civil ceremony. No special wording or vows are needed. The person conducting the ceremony can use a standard script or the couple can write their own vows. However, the couple must at least say that they intend to marry each other.

THE IMPACT OF MARRIAGE

Once you're married, you have many legal rights and legal obligations. Federal and state laws grant married couples benefits. Couples who file their income taxes together pay lower income taxes. A spouse usually doesn't have to pay estate taxes and gift taxes on money received from his or her partner. A noncitizen married to a U.S. citizen gains immigration and residency benefits. Spouses can also share federal benefits, such as Social Security and Medicare. In most instances, a court cannot make a spouse give testimony against his or her spouse if he or she is a defendant in a criminal trial.

Married couples may also receive certain employment benefits, such as health insurance for a spouse who doesn't have insurance and medical leave to care for an ill spouse. A spouse can legally make medical decisions if his or her partner becomes incapacitated. Married couples also enjoy consumer benefits, such as lower family rates for home and auto insurance.

Marriage also results in legal obligations and financial responsibilities. Although the duties differ among states, in general, a married couple is legally required to share income and property acquired during the marriage. Depending on the circumstances, a spouse might continue to have financial responsibilities for his or her spouse in case of a divorce. The couple is also responsible for the care, education, and health of their children. Governments consider both spouses' income and debts when considering taxes owed, inheritance, divorce settlements, and government benefits. Likewise, banks will consider the income and debts of both partners when making decisions about loans and credit.

SAME-SEX MARRIAGE

Although same-sex marriage has been a controversial political and social issue, it is legal in more than one-third of the United States. In these states, people of the same sex can marry, as long as they meet the state's legal requirements for marriage. After marrying, they enjoy the same benefits and have the same legal responsibilities as opposite-sex married couples.

Most states, however, still limit marriage to unions of a man and a woman. Courts have ruled that some of the laws banning same-sex marriage are unconstitutional. Although the opposition to same-sex marriage remains strong in many states, the trend is toward more state legislatures adopting laws that allow same-sex marriage.

DOMESTIC PARTNERSHIPS AND CIVIL UNIONS

A few states that do not allow same-sex marriages have laws recognizing domestic partnerships or civil unions for same-sex couples. A domestic partnership or civil union functions much like a marriage, and usually, both same-sex and heterosexual couples may apply for one. However, no marriage license is required. Instead, the couple files a notarized form with a state office—usually the secretary of state—to register their domestic partnership or civil

Two men show their joy while exchanging marriage vows on a beach. Same-sex marriage is legal in many states, and more states appear likely to legalize gay marriages in the future.

union with the state. To end a civil union or domestic partnership, a couple must go through a court hearing similar to a divorce.

States with domestic-partnership or civil-union laws offer couples limited rights and benefits. Some give same-sex married couples such rights as divorce, alimony, and child custody. Some cities and businesses also recognize domestic partnerships and civil unions. They offer same-sex couples such benefits as health insurance, sick and bereavement leave, accident and life insurance, parental leave, and housing rights. However, domestic partnerships and civil unions do not offer the same range of benefits or require the same level of responsibilities as a marriage.

COMMON-LAW MARRIAGES

Cohabitation, or living together, is an alternative to marriage. Sometimes known as a common-law marriage, cohabitation is defined as two people who live together and accept the rights and obligations traditionally enjoyed by a married couple. However, living together without being legally marriage means that the couple cannot rely on the legal protections or benefits of marriage.

Legal problems often arise when an unmarried couple splits up. Disputes about property, parental rights, and financial issues are common and can be difficult to resolve. For those in a cohabitation relationship, a good solution to avoid problems is to write out a cohabitation agreement. This document, which is a type of contract, will establish legally what each partner wants to happen if the relationship ends.

To create a cohabitation agreement, you and your partner should write out the terms you agree upon. Each partner should sign two copies of the finished document and keep one copy each. Also, make an additional copy and give it to a parent or friend to keep, in case you lose yours. In the agreement, you can agree to anything you want. The document should at least cover how to divide property owned by each partner before you moved in together and how to divide property obtained after you

Both members of an unmarried couple should agree to the terms of a cohabitation agreement. This type of contract helps avoid problems and disputes over property if the couple later separates.

begin living together. It should also address real estate, debts, household expenses, bank accounts and credit cards, and parenting issues. If only one partner is working while the other takes care of the household and children, the document should include an agreement that the employed spouse will pay support to the other spouse in case of a breakup.

Unmarried couples might also want to create other agreements. A health care directive will enable a partner to make medical decisions for the other partner if that person becomes incapacitated. A financial proxy allows one partner to make financial decisions on behalf of the couple. Some unmarried couples create separate wills to ensure that the surviving partner receives the couple's property and custody of their children in case of the death of one partner.

Civil courts will usually treat such agreements as contracts and will enforce the terms of a cohabitation agreement, health directive, or financial proxy made by an unmarried couple. However, there is no legal process similar to a divorce for unmarried couples. Most courts won't divide property or order the payment of support when an unmarried couple splits up. A few states recognize what is known colloquially as palimony, which means that, in those states, a court may distribute property between partners or order one partner in a cohabitation situation to pay support to the other partner. A contract for palimony would only be enforceable if it contained certain necessary elements and if sexual services were not part of the contract.

CHAPTER 2

BREAKING UP IS HARD TO DO

Mr. and Mrs. Warren separated after seven years of marriage. In their divorce, a California court gave each parent joint custody of their two children and divided the children's time equally between the two parents. The parents continued to live in the same city for five years. Now, Mrs. Warren wants to accept a job located about one hundred miles (160 km) away from her current home. She asks a court to give her sole custody of the children. She claims joint custody would disrupt the lives of the children because of the distance between her new home and her ex-husband's home. Mr. Warren opposes his ex-wife's plan to move the children away. He thinks the joint custody arrangement should continue. What are his legal options? What are hers?

DIVORCE BASICS

Couples get married expecting a happy future together. However, more than 40 percent of marriages in the United State end in divorce. A divorce is a court order that legally ends a marriage. The legal requirements of divorce vary from state to state, so you should familiarize yourself with the laws in your state if you're considering a divorce.

Either a husband or a wife may ask a court for a divorce. If both parties want to divorce and have no disagreements about how to divide their joint property and about who will take care of the children (if any), a divorce can be a relatively simple process. Many divorces, however, are complicated, involving major disputes over property, alimony, child custody, or child support.

To get a divorce, you must meet the legal requirements for divorce in your state. Most states require that you have

Constantly arguing over a long period of time may indicate that a couple's marriage has fallen apart. One spouse may claim the disagreements as grounds for a divorce.

lived in the state for a certain amount of time. You can get divorced only in the state where you live. Most states require that you and your spouse be separated, meaning that you live apart, for a specific length of time before divorcing.

Most states also require that you have a good reason for getting divorced. Legal grounds for a divorce include cruel and inhuman treatment (mental and physical abuse or actions that endanger the life or health of the spouse); abandonment (the voluntary renunciation of one's right to property one owns); adultery (voluntary sexual relations with someone other than one's spouse); confinement in prison; or a permanent breakdown in the relationship (which can arise from a number of factors, including personality conflicts, extended physical separation, and constant arguing) that has lasted for a certain period of time.

In most cases, separation is the first stage of divorce. However, some separated couples do not want to get divorced because of financial, religious, or personal reasons. Some states allow legal separations. This means that the couple remains married, but a court makes decisions on many of the same financial and other issues that would be decided in a divorce. The court's order will state that the couple is legally separated.

HOW TO GET DIVORCED

How to approach a divorce depends on the circumstances. Divorces are usually either contested or uncontested. An uncontested divorce means that both parties want to get divorced and agree on all the terms of the divorce. A contested divorce means that the couple disagrees on the issue of getting divorced or they disagree about the terms of the divorce.

Once you've decided to divorce, the first step in the legal process is to figure out which court in your state handles divorces. In most states, it is a state court located in your county or judicial district. For example, in New York, the state's supreme court hears divorce cases. So, if you live in Buffalo, the New York Supreme Court in Erie County will handle your case.

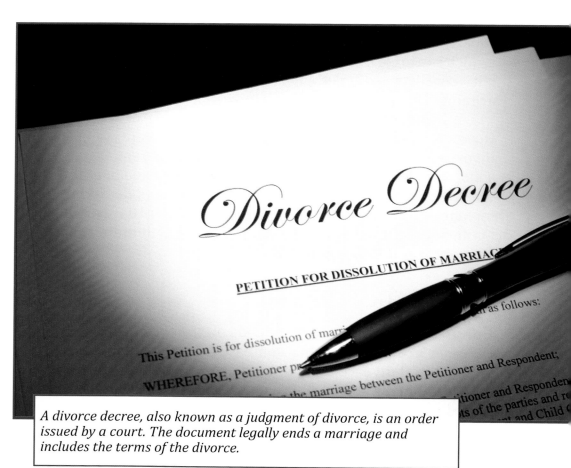

A divorce decree, also known as a judgment of divorce, is an order issued by a court. The document legally ends a marriage and includes the terms of the divorce.

The process of getting a divorce varies by state. For example, in New York, to start a divorce case, you must go to the county clerk's office and pay a fee to get an index number. This number identifies your divorce case. You must also file a summons with the county clerk. This legal document states the reason for the divorce. The summons may also include your requests for the distribution of property, alimony, child custody, child support, and visitation. Next, you must have another person formally deliver the summons to your spouse. The summons notifies your spouse that you have filed for divorce and that he or she is the defendant in the divorce case.

If you are seeking an uncontested divorce, the process might be relatively easy to navigate. You can seek an uncontested divorce if your spouse agrees to the divorce and you and your spouse have no disagreements at all over any financial or divorce-related issue. When making agreements about these issues with your spouse, make sure that the final decisions are fair to both parties. If your spouse ignores the summons and does not show up in court to oppose the divorce, the court will treat it as an uncontested divorce.

If your spouse wants the divorce and agrees to the terms that both of you have negotiated, he or she should sign a form approving the divorce. Then you would submit all of the divorce forms and papers to the court for approval. In some states, courts will grant a divorce without a court hearing. Other states require both parties to be present in a court to finalize a divorce. The judge will sign the judgment of divorce, and the county clerk will record the divorce. The parties are then legally divorced. You can get copies of the judgment of divorce from the county clerk.

If your spouse does not want a divorce or if you cannot agree on all of the terms of the divorce, you will have a contested divorce. The process for a contested divorce is complicated. In most cases, each party should seek legal representation to protect their financial and other interests. If you cannot afford to hire an attorney, community legal-aid clinics and law school legal clinics provide free legal advice and representation. If you make substantially less money than your spouse, ask the court to order your spouse to pay your legal fees.

Although the process varies by state, in most instances a spouse will answer a divorce summons either to oppose the divorce or to dispute the terms of the divorce. He or she will return a form called a notice of appearance to the court. It informs the court that the defendant wants to appear in court to contest the divorce.

Each spouse in a divorce must provide financial statements showing assets and liabilities. A judge will usu- ally hold a preliminary hearing that covers the contested issues involved in the divorce, such as dividing property, alimony payments, and child-related issues. The judge attempts to get the parties to resolve as many issues as possible.

The judge may order reports from experts to deter- mine certain issues. For example, the judge may want a report from a child psychologist who has interviewed the couple's children before making any decisions on child cus- tody. If some issues remain unresolved, the judge will hold

An estranged couple negotiates the terms of a divorce as a lawyer takes notes. Most couples are able to reach a settlement before their divorce goes to court.

a pretrial conference to try to negotiate a final settlement. If unsuccessful, the divorce case will go to trial. In most cases, a settlement is reached before a divorce goes to trial.

At trial, each side presents his or her case. Based on the arguments, expert reports, and evidence presented at trial, the judge will make decisions to settle the unresolved issues. Once a divorce is finalized through a settlement or a trial, the judge signs a judgment of divorce, and the parties are legally divorced.

ANNULMENT

Although divorce is the most common way to dissolve a marriage, an annulment also ends a marriage. Most annulments involve marriages that have lasted only a few weeks or months. This is because an annulment treats the marriage as if it never occurred. Some people choose an annulment to avoid the shame of a divorce. Others seek an annulment so they can remarry in their church. There are two types of annulment: civil and religious.

A state government grants a civil annulment. The grounds for a civil annulment differ from state to state, but most annulment laws require at least one of the following to exist: a spouse must have concealed or lied about something that was essential to the marriage; the marriage has not been consummated, which means no sexual intercourse has occurred; or the union does not satisfy a necessary requirement for a legal marriage, such as one of the partners was underage or was already married.

In most cases, getting an annulment isn't too complicated. You must file for an annulment at a county court. If annulment forms are not available online, you can get them from the court's clerk. Fill out the forms and return them to the court. To finalize the annulment, you must appear before a judge and prove that one of the legal grounds for an annulment is true in your case. If the court agrees that you have met the legal requirements, it will issue an annulment order. This order immediately ends your marriage.

Religious institutions, particularly the Roman Catholic Church, allow couples to get a religious annulment after they obtain a civil divorce. A religious annulment allows a divorced person to remarry within his or her church and have the new marriage recognized by the church. The grounds for a religious annulment might differ from those for a civil annulment. For example, a religious annulment may be granted if one partner lacked the intention to have children or be faithful to his or her spouse. To get a religious annulment, you must meet with a priest or other church official. He will guide you through the process.

CHILD CUSTODY

One of the major issues in many divorces is deciding which spouse gets custody of the couple's child or children. This is the issue that often causes the most conflict. Custody is a parent's legal right to control his or her child's upbringing. It gives a parent the right to make major decisions about a child's education, religion, and health.

In a divorce case, both parents may ask for custody of their children under age eighteen. You must include the name, birth date, and other information identifying the child in your divorce papers. You also must ask the court to give you custody of your children in your divorce papers. Custody does not automatically go to either the mother or the father.

Your spouse might agree to let you have custody, and your divorce judgment will indicate that you have legal custody of the child. If you and your spouse cannot agree on custody, the judge handling your case will decide who gets custody. The judge will base the custody decision on the best interests of the child. He or she will consider many factors, including which parent has been the child's primary

VISITATION

If one parent has sole custody of a child, the other parent might have visitation rights. You and your former spouse can agree to a visitation schedule. If your spouse is refusing to let you visit with your child, you can file a court case to request a visitation order. Courts will usually allow the parent without custody to have scheduled visits with the child. A court may refuse to issue a visitation order if you have a past history of child abuse or if there is some other issue that would threaten the best interests of the child.

Most parents who do not have custody of their children have visitation rights, which allow them to visit their children or have their children stay with them temporarily, often on a set schedule.

caretaker, the environment of each parent's home, and the financial, mental, and physical fitness of each parent. Other considerations include with which parent the child has been residing and with which parent the child wants to reside. The judge may give custody of all the children to one parent or may give each parent custody of different children. The judge may also decide to grant joint custody. This means that the two parents must make major decisions about the child together. Minor decisions are usually made by the parent who is caring for the child at the time.

CHILD SUPPORT

In all states, divorced or separated parents have a legal obligation to support their children.

Child support is money paid by one divorced or separated parent to another for a child's housing, food, clothing, and other living expenses.

Like other issues involved in a divorce, the two parents can agree to the terms of child support during the divorce proceedings. If a divorcing couple is unable to agree to the amount of support or if the parents are separated and not divorced yet, a parent can ask a court to order the other parent to pay child support. Most states have legal guidelines for determining the amount of child support. The amount depends on the income of each parent and how much each parent spends on the child's expenses. A court can increase or decrease a child-support order if a parent's financial circumstances or other factors change.

Once a divorce settlement or court order establishes an obligation to pay child support, the payments must be made. If your spouse is not paying child support, your state or local child-support service office can help you collect child support. These organizations act on behalf of the state to make sure children receive the financial support they need. You can also get help collecting money owed by hiring an attorney.

A court can order child support funds deducted from a parent's wages. The money is taken from the parent's paycheck by the state and sent to the parent owed child support. States can also intercept a federal tax refund to cover late or missing child-support payments. In some states, a parent who is delinquent on child-support payments can lose his or her driver's license or professional license. The federal government may prevent a parent who owes back child support from renewing his or her passport. A court can also issue a contempt of court order against the parent. The parent will pay a fine or serve jail time.

Some states have made failure to make child-support payments a crime. For example, Indiana Code 35-46-1-5 makes nonsupport of a child a Level 6 felony if a person knowingly or intentionally fails to provide support to a dependent child. It's a Level 5 felony if the amount of unpaid support owed is $15,000 or more. Under Indiana law, a Level 6 felony is punishable by six months to three years in prison or a fine of $10,000. A Level 5 felony is punishable by two to eight years in prison or a fine of $10,000. If you are charged with a nonsupport-of-a-child crime, showing that you're financially unable to provide support is a valid defense.

CHAPTER 3

AND BABY MAKES THREE

Sixteen-year-old Cody D. received a letter from an Illinois adoption agency telling him that he had been named the father of a child. It instructed him to hire an attorney if he wanted to parent the child. Months earlier, Cody's ex-girlfriend had texted him that she was pregnant. He figured that she or her friends were just messing with him. She never mentioned the pregnancy again. He noticed that she wore loose clothes to school, but she didn't look pregnant.

A few weeks after Cody received the letter, his ex-girlfriend gave birth to their child. She had approached the adoption agency because she wanted the child to have a mother and a father. Cody soon found out that the adoption agency had placed the baby with an adoptive family. Cody wants to get the baby back from the adoptive family and raise the child himself. What should he do?

PREGNANCY AND ABORTION

While having a child is a joyful prospect for many people, it also creates legal rights and responsibilities. Prospective parents, as well as couples who already have children, need to be aware of the laws that apply before and after their child is born.

If you are pregnant, you might wish to terminate the pregnancy for a number of reasons. Abortion is a medical procedure performed by a licensed doctor or health-care professional that is intended to end a pregnancy. There is also an abortion pill that will end a pregnancy. Abortion has been legal in the United States since 1973. However, states have adopted various regulations regarding abortion, so abortion laws differ greatly from state to state. More than forty states prohibit abortion after a certain point in a pregnancy, unless an abortion is necessary to protect a woman's life. This cutoff is usually either twenty or twenty-four weeks after conception, depending on state law. About one-third of the states require a woman seeking an abortion to receive counseling before the medical procedure takes place. About half of the states require a waiting period after the counseling session, usually twenty-four hours.

If you are considering having an abortion, research abortion laws to find out the restrictions in your state. Consult with your doctor or a local women's health clinic. Both can provide information and guidance about medical and emotional issues, as well as legal restrictions.

PARENTS AND THEIR RIGHTS

When a child is born, the mother has sole legal custody of the newborn. In almost all cases, it's clear that she's the child's mother. The same cannot be said for the father. In general, a woman's husband is presumed to be the father of her child. To gain shared custody of the child, the husband

A mother has sole legal custody of a child until the father is named, either through a formal acknowledgment by the father or by a paternity test.

must sign a state form acknowledging that he is the father of the child (often, the father's signature on the baby's birth certificate is enough).

When an unmarried woman has a child, the new-born does not have a legal father until paternity is established. In most states, a mother and the father can sign a form acknowledging that the man is the father of the child. If either the mother or the father refuses to sign the form, a paternity lawsuit might be necessary to establish who is the father.

31

PATERNITY TEST

DNA testing is common in cases in which a child's paternity needs to be determined. It is usually done by collecting cells from inside a man's cheek using a cotton swab. This test will show either that the man is almost certainly the child's biological father or that he is absolutely not the biological father. To get a paternity test, contact your county child services office or a private genetic-testing lab.

Cheek cells contain a person's DNA. A genetics lab can use DNA in a paternity test to establish whether the person tested is most likely the biological father of a child.

If you're the mother of a child born out of wedlock and want to make the biological father financially responsible for the child, you can file a paternity suit. Likewise, if you think you are the father of a child born out of wedlock, you can file a paternity suit to ensure your parental rights. Paternity issues are complicated and require professional help. Seek guidance from your local child-services department. Hire an attorney who specializes in family law or, if you cannot afford an attorney, seek free legal assistance from a community legal clinic or law school legal clinic.

Once the father is identified, a court can issue orders covering a range of parenting issues, based on the best interest of the child. A judge can order the father to pay the mother's pregnancy and birth expenses and pay ongoing child support. The judge can also grant the father custody or visitation rights.

Parents have the right to make important decisions and take certain actions on behalf of their child. Although state laws on parental rights differ, most statutes seek to ensure the best interests of the child. Parental rights include the right to make health care and other major decisions for the child, enter into a contract on behalf of the child, and visit the child.

INVOLUNTARY TERMINATION OF PARENTAL RIGHTS

All states allow their courts to end a parent-child relationship when certain conditions are met. Once this legal relationship has been terminated, the child may be adopted.

The termination of parental rights can be involuntary or voluntary.

An involuntary termination is usually based on the parent or parents' mistreatment of the child or their inability to care for the child. Common factors include significant child abuse or neglect, sexual abuse, failure to support the child, or the parent's physical or mental illness. Most state laws require a court to rule that there is clear and convincing evidence that the parents are unfit and that terminating parental rights is in the best interest of the child. An involuntary termination can end the rights of one parent but not affect the rights of the other parent. If a court terminates the rights of both parents, a state agency takes custody of the child and seeks to find a permanent home with adoptive parents. A voluntary termination of parental rights occurs when parents agree to give up their parental rights. It usually results in an adoption.

ADOPTION

Adoption is the process in which an adult legally becomes the guardian of a child and assumes the rights and responsibilities of being the child's parent. Some states have open adoptions, meaning that the mother can select the adoptive parents. Others allow only closed adoptions. The mother must give up all parental rights to the child, and a state agency selects the adoptive parents. Some states permit both types of adoptions.

Most states don't allow a child's parents to agree to an adoption until the child is born. If you're having a baby and want to offer it for adoption, research the laws in your

People seeking to adopt a child will have to prove they can provide a safe and secure home once a match has been identified.

state before your child is born. Contact the agency in your state responsible for adoptions or a private adoption agency to get the information you need. After the baby is born, the mother—and in some cases the father—must sign a consent form. Some states require a waiting period of a few days before the parents can sign this form. By signing the consent-to-adoption form, you give up all parental rights to your child.

If you want to adopt a baby, you should register as a prospective adoptive parent with a state agency or independent adoption agency. Once the agency has an appropriate child available for adoption, it will conduct a home study. A social worker will visit your home and gather information about your marriage, job, finances, and other relevant data. Don't stress. Just be yourself. The worker will write a report summarizing your suitability as a parent. The report will either give you a positive or negative recommendation.

In all states, a court must approve an adoption. You must file an adoption petition with a court to request approval for the adoption. You must give notice to the child's parents, the adoption agency, and any other person or organization required to consent to the adoption under state law. At the adoption hearing, the judge considers the social worker's report and other information to decide whether the adoption is in the best interest of the child. If the judge approves the adoption, the court will issue a final decree of adoption. This document legalizes your adoption. You now have all the legal rights and responsibilities of a parent.

MINORS AND HEALTH CARE ISSUES

Parents have the legal authority to make medical decisions for their children under age eighteen. However, in certain cases, minors have the right to make their own decisions involving certain types of health care. Many states have laws that permit minors to get contraceptives, prenatal care, mental-health services, and treatment for sexually transmitted infections without parental involvement. These laws aim to encourage minors to seek medical care for health issues that they might not wish to share with their parents.

In many states, these minor-consent laws apply to all minors age twelve or older. Some states, however, allow only specific groups of minors—typically those who are married or who are pregnant—to consent to

Some states allow teenagers to seek certain types of health care without a parent's permission so that they can receive appropriate medical advice or treatment in confidence.

these types of health care services. Some states have no minor-consent laws. They leave it up to individual doctors and health care workers to decide whether to provide these types of medical services to minors without parental consent. If you're a minor and need these medical services but do not want your parents involved, research the minor-consent laws in your state. Also, ask your doctor, school nurse, guidance counselor, or other trusted adult for information and advice.

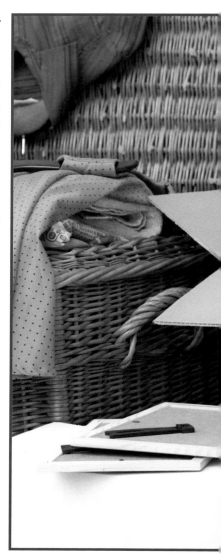

In general, minor-consent laws do not apply to abortion services. Only a few states allow minors to consent to an abortion. Most states require either the consent or notification—or both consent and notification—of at least one parent.

THE EMANCIPATION OF MINORS

Parents are usually responsible for supporting their child until the age of eighteen. Some minors want to be free of their parents' care before they reach this age. State laws determine the rules and procedures for minors seeking independence from their parents. Parents can also seek to emancipate their own children so they no longer have to support them, but that happens only in rare circumstances.

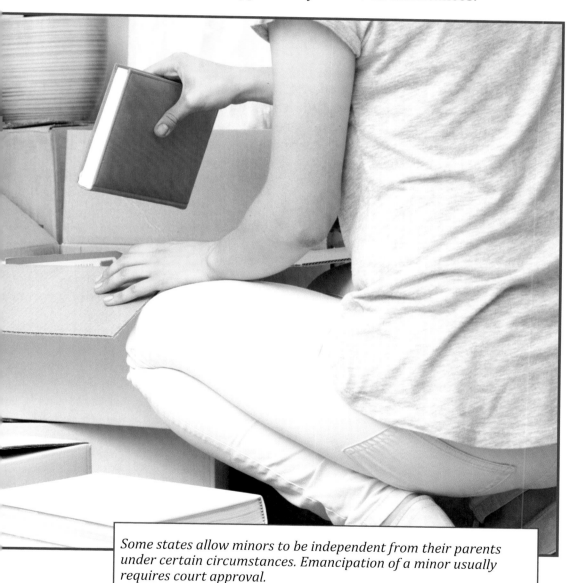

Some states allow minors to be independent from their parents under certain circumstances. Emancipation of a minor usually requires court approval.

Some states allow minors to be emancipated when they get married or join the armed services. In most cases, emancipation requires a court order. If you want to be emancipated from your parents, you must file a petition explaining to a court why you seek independence. In most states, you must notify your parents that you have filed a petition for emancipation. The next step is usually a hearing. The judge will ask you and your parents questions and hear evidence concerning whether emancipation is in your best interests. Courts usually require minors to show that they are financially able to support themselves. If the judge decides in your favor, the court will issue a declaration of emancipation. You will need copies of this document to show landlords, doctors, and others who would normally ask for parental consent before providing services.

Emancipated minors basically have the same legal status as adults. They can make their own decisions about where to live and can enter into legal contracts. Some limitations apply, however. An emancipated minor might still be subject to state laws concerning school attendance, parental consent for marriages and abortions, and age limits for getting a driver's license and buying alcohol.

CHAPTER 4

A BROKEN HOME

Tina began dating Steve in high school. Steve soon started trying to control everything Tina did. He accused her of going out with other guys when all she did was go to the mall. He often got angry with her about little things she did wrong. He always apologized, telling Tina that it wouldn't happen again and that he loved her. Tina married Steve, but she eventually left him because of his controlling behaviors. She moved to Texas to stay with her father. Steve tracked her down and convinced her to return home. Her father drove the couple back to their home in Georgia. As soon as her father left, Steve beat up Tina for leaving him. If you were in Tina's situation, what you do?

DOMESTIC VIOLENCE

Domestic violence is a pattern of abusive behavior that one partner in a relationship uses to gain or keep control over the other partner. It can happen between partners who are married, living together, or dating. Domestic violence affects people from all social and economic backgrounds. Children who are exposed to domestic violence are more likely to have physical or emotional problems. They also

Sometimes a conflict in a relationship leads to domestic violence. If you or a friend are the victim of domestic violence, seek help immediately from law enforcement and community domestic-violence organizations.

grow up to believe that violence in a relationship is normal, increasing the risk that, as an adult, they will become either an abuser or a domestic-violence victim as an adult.

Domestic violence is not limited to physical and sexual abuse. Emotional abuse occurs when one partner damages the other's sense of self-worth. Threatening physical harm, destroying property, and keeping a partner apart from friends and family are signs of psychological abuse. Economic abuse includes making a partner financially dependent by controlling the couple's finances or by preventing a partner from working or attending school.

All states have domestic-violence laws that prohibit physical abuse, threats of physical abuse, and sexual abuse. Some states also outlaw emotional or psychological abuse or financial mistreatment. If you or someone you know is a victim of domestic violence, get help. In the event of physical or sexual abuse, dial 911 to summon the police. In many states, police are required to arrest a person suspected of physical or sexual abuse of a partner.

Also seek assistance if you or someone else is a victim of other types of domestic violence. Call the National Domestic Violence Hotline at 1-800-799-SAFE, the National Coalition Against Domestic Violence at 1-303-839-1852,

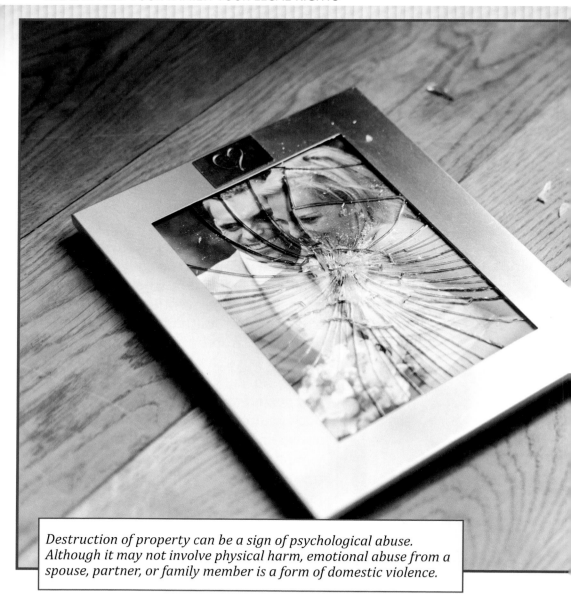

Destruction of property can be a sign of psychological abuse. Although it may not involve physical harm, emotional abuse from a spouse, partner, or family member is a form of domestic violence.

the National Victim Center at 1-800-FYI-CALL, or the National Organization for Victim Assistance at 1-800-TRY-NOVA.

Women's shelters, rape crisis centers, and state and community domestic-violence organizations and programs provide local assistance. These groups provide temporary shelter, legal advice and representation, counseling, and other services.

In most states, a victim of domestic violence can get a protective order. This court order prohibits further abuse and contact with the victim. It bans the abuser from the victim's home, school, or workplace. A protective order might make the abuser pay spousal or child support. The court may also order the abuser to participate in domestic-violence counseling. Any violation of the order will most likely result in legal action. Depending on the state, a protective order lasts anywhere from three months to five years. When it ends, you can go back to court to get a new protective order, if necessary. A protective order should be used only in cases in which abuse or the fear of abuse exists; it should never be used simply to gain an advantage over a partner in an argument or other circumstance.

CHILD ABUSE AND NEGLECT

Child abuse is any type of abuse or neglect of a child under age eighteen by a parent, caregiver, or a person who has temporary responsibility for the child, such as a teacher or a minister. Like domestic violence, child abuse isn't just physical mistreatment. It also includes emotional abuse, such as constantly ridiculing or humiliating a child; frequently screaming at or threatening a child; showing a child no affection or attention; allowing others to abuse a child; or telling a child that he or she is "no good" or was a "mistake." Child sexual abuse includes fondling, intercourse, producing child pornography, or any other sexual act involving an adult and a child.

Child neglect occurs when a parent consistently fails to provide for a child's basic needs. It includes not providing a child food, clothing, and other physical needs. Isolating a child from contact with relatives, friends, and other people or failing to enroll the child in school is also considered child neglect.

Signs of emotional child abuse include a child showing little or no attachment to a parent, being overly withdrawn, or being excessively worried about doing something wrong. Signs of physical child abuse include recurring or unexplained injuries, fearful behavior, aggression, and wearing clothing out of season to cover injuries. Signs of child neglect include inadequate medical care, frequent absences from school, clothes that are dirty, the wrong size, or inappropriate for the weather, and noticeable body odor or other grooming issues.

To grow up healthy and happy, children need consistency and structure, as well as the assurance that their

INFANT ABANDONMENT

Some mothers and parents—particularly young, unmarried ones—choose to abandon their newborns. Sometimes, the infant is left to die. All states have laws to provide a safe and confidential means to give up an unwanted infant. Known as safe haven or safe surrender laws, they allow a parent to give up an infant if certain requirements are met. The infant must be a certain age, ranging from under seventy-two hours old to as much as one year old. The parent can surrender the infant only at specific locations. Hospitals, firehouses, police stations, and licensed adoption agencies are common places legally designated as safe havens. Some infant abandonment statutes guarantee that no questions will be asked and that parents do not have to give their names. The National Safe Haven Alliance has a safe-haven locator on its website: http://www.nationalsafehavenalliance.org/states.

parent is looking out for them. Abused children cannot predict how a parent will act. They feel scared, uncared for, and alone. Child abuse often has long-lasting effects. It harms a young person's ability to have healthy relationships and participate in family life or at school. Victims of child abuse often feel worthless, have trouble controlling their emotions, and distrust other people.

If you are the victim of child abuse or neglect, or if you suspect a child is being abused or neglected, the legal system can help. For immediate help to stop the physical abuse of a child, dial 911 to summon police. For other types of child abuse, contact the child services agency in your state that investigates cases of child abuse or neglect. The counselors at the Childhelp

In an effort to stop child abuse and keep families together, state agencies offer counseling services to parents involved in child abuse cases.

National Child Hotline, 800-4-A-CHILD, can also refer you to social-service and support resources in your community.

In a case of child abuse or neglect, a state agency may remove a child from the home. The agency will temporarily place the child in the care of a relative, foster home, or state shelter. The agency will try to resolve a case of abuse or neglect by addressing the causes of the problem. They will provide the parent with counseling, public assistance, job training, or other social services. The agency's goal is to reunite the family and avoid future abuse or neglect of the child. In extreme cases of child abuse or neglect, the state agency may ask a court to terminate an abusive parent's parental rights. A court may issue an order ending the parent-child relationship, making the child available for adoption.

A person who abuses or neglects a child might also be subject to criminal charges. All states have laws that prohibit child abuse and neglect. Penalties for child abuse, particularly sexual abuse, can be harsh and include long prison sentences. If you have been charged with child abuse or neglect, you will need legal counsel to deal with the charges. If you cannot afford to hire a lawyer, you have the right to a free, court-appointed attorney.

CHILD ABDUCTION

There are three types of child abduction. A family abduction occurs when a family member kidnaps a child. This is the most common type of child abduction. A family abduction is usually committed by a parent who does not have custody of the child and usually involves a child under the age of six. An acquaintance abduction is committed by someone known to the child or parents. It often involves teenaged victims and perpetrators. A stranger abduction is committed by a person unknown to the child or parents. It is usually committed away from the home and is often associated with sexual assaults.

If your child has been abducted, contact your local police immediately. They may issue an Amber Alert, which informs the public that a child has been abducted in the area. Kidnapping, including, in most states, the abduction of a child by a parent, is a serious crime. Kidnapping is both a state and federal crime. The FBI may investigate an abduction if there is reason to suspect the abductor took the child across state lines or fled to another country with the child. A conviction could result in a prison sentence.

Turning to the legal system can be daunting, especially when intimate family dynamics are on the line. But damaged family relations do not have to affect your whole life. Understanding the fundamentals of family law can give you the tools to rise above destructive problems, craft a better future for yourself and your loved ones, and guard against potential issues.

GLOSSARY

adoption A legal proceeding in which an adult takes custody of a child who is not the adult's natural offspring.

annulment A court declaration that a marriage was never valid.

child abuse Any physical, sexual, or psychological maltreatment of a child by a parent or other person who is responsible for the child's welfare.

child neglect Failure by a parent to provide appropriate care to a child that threatens the child's well-being.

child support Money paid by one parent to another, after separation or divorce, for a child's expenses.

cohabitation Sharing a home with, and usually having a sexual relationships with, another person. Also sometimes known as common-law marriage.

common-law marriage An arrangement in which an unmarried couple lives together as if they were married. Also sometimes known as cohabitation.

contested divorce A divorce proceeding in which one spouse opposes the divorce or proposed terms of the divorce.

court order A direction of the court that must be obeyed.

custody The right to control a child's care and the duty to provide care to the child.

divorce The ending of a marriage by a court order.

domestic violence A pattern of physical, sexual, or psychological attacks committed by one family member on another.

emancipation The legal release of a child from the control and responsibility of a parent.

joint custody When separated or divorced parents have equal rights to control a child's care and equal duties to provide care to the child.

judgment of divorce A document signed by a court granting a divorce.

marriage The act, ceremony, or formal proceeding by which a couple becomes spouses.

paternity The state or condition of being a father; the establishment of a legal father and child relationship.

paternity order A court order that states who is the legal father of a child.

petition A written request to a court asking it to issue a specific order, such as an order of child support or an order of visitation.

protective order In the context of family law, a court order that protects a person, such as the victim of domestic violence, from another person.

separation The absence of one spouse from a married couple's home usually prior to a divorce.

settlement An agreement that all the issues in a legal dispute, such as a divorce, have been negotiated and resolved.

summons A legal document notifying the named person that a lawsuit or other legal proceeding, such as a divorce, has been filed.

termination of parental rights A signed consent form or court order that ends the parental rights of a birth parent, often enabling a child to be adopted.

uncontested divorce A divorce in which both spouses agree to the divorce and the terms of the divorce, or a divorce in which one spouse fails to appear in a divorce proceeding.

visitation The right of a parent who does not have custody to be with his or her child.

Canadian Bar Association
National Family Law Section
500-865 Carling Avenue
Ottawa, ON K1S 5S8
Canada
(800) 267-8860
Website: http://www.cba.org/CBA/sections_family/main
This professional association of Canadian lawyers provides
information on issues related to family law in Canada.

Canadian Centre for Child Protection
615 Academy Road
Winnipeg, MB R3N 0E7
Canada
(800) 532-9135
Website: http://www.protectchildren.ca
This charitable organization provides programs and ser-
vices to ensure the safety of Canadian children.

Childhelp
4350 E. Camelback Road, Building F250
Phoenix, AZ 85018
(480) 922-8212
Website: http://www.childhelp.org
This nonprofit organization provides information on the
prevention and treatment of child abuse.

Gay & Lesbian Advocates & Defenders
30 Winter Street, Suite 800
Boston, MA 02108
(617) 426-1350

Website: http://www.glad.org/rights/infoline
This nonprofit provides legal information on same-sex
    marriage and other issues affecting gay and lesbian
    families.

Guttmacher Institute
125 Maiden Lane
7th floor
New York, NY 10038
(212) 248-1111
Website: http://www.guttmacher.org
This nonprofit organization conducts research on and pro-
    vides information about sexual and reproductive health.

National Center for Missing and Exploited Children
699 Prince Street
Alexandria, VA 22314-3175
(800) 843-5678
Website: http://www.missingkids.com
This nonprofit organization works with law enforcement,
    families, and others on issues related to missing and
    sexually exploited children.

National Coalition Against Domestic Violence
One Broadway, Suite B210
Denver, CO 80203
(303) 839-1852
Website: http://www.ncadv.org
This nonprofit organization provides information on
    domestic violence and educates the public on how to
    recognize and take action against domestic violence.

Prevent Child Abuse
228 South Wabash Avenue
10th Floor
Chicago, IL 60604
(312) 663-3520
Website: http://www.preventchildabuse.org
This nonprofit organization provides information on child
    abuse and its prevention.

U.S. Department of Health and Human Services
Office of Child Support Enforcement
370 L'Enfant Promenade SW
Washington, DC 20447
(202) 401-9373
Website: http://www.acf.hhs.gov/programs/css
This federal agency provides information on child support
    and child-support enforcement.

WEBSITES

Because of the changing nature of Internet links, Rosen
Publishing has developed an online list of websites related
to the subject of this book. This site is updated regularly.
Please use this link to access the list:

http://www.rosenlinks.com/KYR/Fami

FOR FURTHER READING

Benrey, Ronald M. *Know Your Rights: A Survival Guide for Non-Lawyers.* New York, NY: Sterling, 2011.

Bergin, Rory M. and Jared Meyer. *Frequently Asked Questions About Divorce.* New York, NY: Rosen, 2012.

Brown, Tracy. *Frequently Asked Questions About Same-Sex Marriage and When a Parent Is Gay.* New York, NY: Rosen, 2013.

Bryfonski, Dedria, ed. *Opposing Viewpoints: Child Custody.* Farmington Hills, MI: Greenhaven, 2011.

Doskow, Emily. *Nolo's Essential Guide to Child Custody & Support.* Berkeley, CA: Nolo, 2013.

Doskow, Emily, and Marcia Stewart. *The Legal Answer Book for Families.* Berkeley, CA: Nolo, 2011.

Duncan, Roderic. *A Judge's Guide to Divorce.* Berkeley, CA: Nolo, 2007.

Farrell, Courtney. *Children's Rights.* Edina, MN: ABDO, 2010.

Ferguson, Olivia, and Hayley Mitchell Haugen, eds. *Age of Consent.* Farmington Hills, MI: Greenhaven, 2010.

Jacobs, Thomas *A. What Are My Rights?: Q&A About Teens and the Law.* Minneapolis, MN: Free Spirit, 2011.

Kenney, Karen Latchana. *Domestic Violence.* Edina, MN: ABDO, 2012.

Kiesbye, Stefan, ed. *Child Abuse and Neglect.* Farmington Hills, MI: Greenhaven, 2008.

Lange, Donna. *Contraception & Pregnancy.* Broomall, PA: Mason Crest, 2014.

Lapidus, Lenora M. et al. *The Rights of Women.* New York, NY: New York University Press, 2009.

Merino, Noël. *Abortion.* Farmington Hills, MI: Greenhaven, 2012.

Peterman, Rosie L. et al. *Divorce and Stepfamilies.* New York, NY: Rosen, 2013.

Pierceson, Jason. *Same-Sex Marriage in the United States.* Lanham, MD: Rowman & Littlefield, 2013.

Sember, Brette McWhorter. *The Divorce Organizer & Planner.* Chicago, IL: McGraw-Hill, 2014.

Stoner, Katherine E. *Divorce Without Court: A Guide to Mediation and Collaborative Divorce.* Berkeley, CA: Nolo, 2012.

Willis, Laurie, ed. *Adoption.* Farmington Hills, MI: Greenhaven, 2012.

BIBLIOGRAPHY

Berry, Dawn Bradley. *The Divorce Sourcebook.* New York, NY: McGraw-Hill, 2007.

California Child Abduction Task Force. "California Child Safety AMBER Network." Revised May 10, 2010. Retrieved April 30, 2014 (http://www.childabductions.org).

Champlin, Joseph M. "Ten Questions About Annulment." Retrieved April 28, 2014 (http://www.americancatholic.org/newsletters/cu/ac1002.asp).

Federal Bureau of Investigation. "Family Child Abductions." Retrieved on April 30, 2013 (http://www.fbi.gov/about-us/investigate/vc_majorthefts/cac/family-abductions).

Gay & Lesbian Advocates & Defenders. "Civil Marriage v. Civil Unions: What's the Difference?" Revised March 2014. Retrieved on April 28, 2014 (http://www.glad.org/uploads/docs/publications/cu-vs-marriage.pdf).

Guttmacher Institute. "Minors' Access to Contraceptive Services." Retrieved April 29, 2014 (http://www.guttmacher.org/statecenter/spibs/spib_MACS.pdf).

Helpguide. "Child Abuse & Neglect." Retrieved May 1, 2014 (http://www.helpguide.org/mental/child_abuse_physical_emotional_sexual_neglect.htm).

Her Justice. "Getting a Divorce in New York." Retrieved April 28, 2014 (http://www.herjustice.org/assets/pdfs/TheBasicsSeries_English/Getting-a-Divorce_ENGLISH.pdf).

Indiana Legislative Services Agency. "Indiana Code 35-46-1-6: Nonsupport of a Dependent Child." Retrieved May 1, 2014 (http://www.in.gov/legislative/ic/code/title35/ar46/ch1.html).

Jasper, Margaret C. *Marriage and Divorce.* New York, NY: Oceana, 2008.

Johnson, Joe. "A view of violence: Survivors share how they overcame abusive relationships." Revised March 23, 2013. Retrieved May 1, 2014 (http://newsle.com/article/0/66464421).

Johnston, Susan. "First Comes Love, Then Comes House? More Unmarried Couples Are Buying Homes." *U.S. News & World Report.* February 25, 2014. Retrieved April 29, 2014 (http://money.usnews.com/money/personal-finance/articles/2014/02/25/first-comes-love-then-comes-house-more-unmarried-couples-are-buying-homes).

KTVI. "Teen Dad Says Adoption Agency Stands in the Way of Raising His Baby." Retrieved April 30, 2014 (http://fox2now.com/2014/04/28/teen-dad-says-adoption-agency-stands-in-the-way-of-raising-his-baby).

LawHelpMN. "Unmarried Fathers' Guide to Paternity, Custody, Parenting Time and Child Support in Minnesota." Revised January 2011. Retrieved April 30, 2014 (http://www.lawhelpmn.org/files/1765CC5E-1EC9-4FC4-65EC-957272D8A04E/attachments/07070DB2-EE7E-2AC7-6EF4-8FEB19549664/365081UnmarriedFathers Guide.pdf).

Missouri Bar. "Family Law Resource Guide." Retrieved April 28, 2014 (https://www.mobar.org/uploadedFiles/Home/Publications/Legal_Resources/Brochures_and_Booklets/Family_Law_Conference/family%20law%20resource%20guide.pdf).

New York Civil Liberties Union. "Teenagers, Health Care & the Law." Retrieved April 29, 2014 (http://www.nyclu.org/files/thl.pdf).

New York State Office for the Prevention of Domestic Violence. "Courts and the Legal System." Retrieved May 1, 2014 (http://www.opdv.ny.gov/professionals/criminal_justice/courts_legalsystem/index.html).

New York Unified Court System. "Introduction to Uncontested Divorce Instructions." Revised April 27, 2014. Retrieved April 30, 2014 (https://www.nycourts.gov/DIVORCE/pdfs/Divorce-Packet-Instructions.pdf).

Office on Child Abuse and Neglect. "Child Neglect: A Guide for Prevention, Assessment and Intervention." 2006. Retrieved April 30, 2014 (https://www.childwelfare.gov/pubs/usermanuals/neglect/chaptertwo.cfm).

Oliphant, Robert E. and Nancy Ver Steegh. *Examples & Explanations: Family Law.* New York, NY: Aspen, 2013.

Pardeck, John T. *Children's Rights: Policy and Practice.* New York, NY: Haworth, 2006.

U.S. Department of Justice. "Domestic Violence." Revised March 2013. Retrieved May 1, 2014 (http://www.ovw.usdoj.gov/domviolence.htm).

U.S. Department of Justice. "Federal Domestic Violence Laws." Retrieved May 1, 2014 (http://www.justice.gov/usao/gan/documents/federallaws.pdf).

Weisberg, D. Kelly. *Emanuel Law Outlines: Family Law.* New York, NY: Aspen, 2011.

INDEX

ABOUT THE AUTHOR

G. S. Prentzas has written more than thirty books for young readers, including *Essential Careers as a Paralegal and Legal Assistant* for Rosen. He also writes articles on legal topics for Lawyers.com, LegalZoom.com, and other websites. He graduated from the University of North Carolina with a bachelor of arts degree with honors in English and from the University of North Carolina School of Law with a juris doctor degree with honors.

ABOUT THE EXPERT REVIEWER

Lindsay A. Lewis, Esq., is a practicing criminal defense attorney in New York City, where she handles a wide range of matters, from those discussed in this series to high-profile federal criminal cases. She believes that each and every defendant deserves a vigorous and informed defense. Ms. Lewis is a graduate of the Benjamin N. Cardozo School of Law and Vassar College.

PHOTO CREDITS

Cover © iStockphoto.com/cgering (teen), © iStockphoto.com/4774344sean (adults); cover background Christophe Rolland/Shutterstock; p. 4–5 Jupiterimages/Polka Dot/Thinkstock; p. 8 Hill Street Studios/Blend Images/Thinkstock; p. 10 Digital Vision/Photodisc/Thinkstock; p. 13 ArrowStudio/Shutterstock.com; p. 15 © iStockphoto.com/Jodi Jacobson; p. 18 wavebreakmedia/Shutterstock.com; p. 20 zimmytws/Shutterstock.com; p. 23 Oredia Eurl/SuperStock; p. 26 Burger/Phanie/SuperStock; p. 31 Zurijeta/Shutterstock.com; p. 32 Wavebreakmedia Ltd/Thinkstock; p. 35 Jupiterimages/Pixland/Thinkstock; pp. 37, 48–49 monkeybusinessimages/iStock/Thinkstock; pp. 38–39 KatarzynaBialasiewicz/iStock/Thinkstock; pp. 42–43 Peter Bernik/Shutterstock.com; pp. 44–45 Twin Design/Shutterstock.com.

Designer: Brian Garvey; Editor: Shalini Saxena